# Time Struggles?

Don Barnes

Published by Don Barnes, 2024.

# Table of Contents

# About the Author

Don is the founder and author of Life Works in Threes!™ E-books. He is a lifelong Texan who has traveled extensively while taking a keen interest in human behavior. His curiosity about life and what drives humans led him to the discovery of how life works in threes. He coined this term as the *Tryune Concept*.

Don attended college on an athletic scholarship and then embarked on a 30-year career in the oil and gas industry. Since the year 2000, he has been a consultant for distributors and manufacturers of various industries. Along the way, he worked on his Tryune discovery in hopes of someday sharing his findings with those struggling unnecessarily... in life. What Don surmised from 40+ years of R&D was that people were struggling unnecessarily because they were not aware that "life works in threes." They, for the most part, have been living their lives <u>by chance</u> rather than <u>by choice,</u> he also discovered.

From this, he began focusing on the "mechanics of life" which shows formulas for success with subjects such as *life, health, money, purpose and so forth*. When people are able to grasp the Tryune Concept, they can apply the formulas with topics that interest them and begin eliminating the struggle. This epiphany is what triggered his Tryune venture and is now on the path of sharing with all who desire to improve on their lives.

Don currently resides in Southern California and Texas while overseeing his businesses and investments.

## Life Works in Threes™

When I was a kid growing up, no one sat me down and said, "Okay Don, I'm going to show you how life works so that you can navigate your way through adulthood." I graduated from school, got married and went about my way with the "learn as you go" concept. It was kind of like putting together a backyard swing set without a set of instructions. Lots of frustration and do-overs, for sure!

My discovery of the "triune" word and noticing how things come together in threes is really what set me off on researching that maybe "life comes in three" …sort of a mechanical approach to managing life, if you will. I combed the libraries and bookstores for information on this and found one book on the subject that was written back in 1951. The author's name was John S. Arant.

What Mr. Arant had to say is this "For lack of a better name, I have called this *The Triangle of Triumph* and therefore, consistent with the name, since most of these conclusions are built on the geometric figure of the triangle." He continued "All Life and all lives are seated in, and circumscribed by, the triangle. The Author and Source and Director of all life is Himself triune in character – Father, Son, and Holy Spirit. Man is of triple nature – body, mind, and spirit – and within those three there are many triangles – desires, development, decay; intellect, will, sensibilities. Of this "paced interlude in the midst of eternity" which we call time there is the triangle of Past, Present, and Future. Space – that limitless and measureless element of the physical universe – is best known in terms of Height, Breadth, and Depth. Try building yourself some triangles along the lines of your Will, your Work, your Way – You will find some interesting angles.

So, for the first time, I realized that life is designed in a mechanical way to come in threes. That means you don't have to rely on wishing and hoping things turn out okay. You can actually look at the three parts that a particular thing is made of and then apply them to get what you're wanting. Like a three-ingredient recipe or a combination lock. With a combination lock, you need the three exact numbers to unlock the lock...otherwise you will continue to struggle.

Some 40 years later, I accumulated things that work in threes and that's when I knew I needed to share this with anyone wanting answers. To have success/harmony in your life, just apply the three parts of an area you're working on, and things will fall into place. I also learned that the recipe for success with just about anything is by doing these three things, consistently – THINK positively, SPEAK positively and ACT positively. For example, if I want to be a successful artist. I would think to myself "I can do this because I have the talent." Then I would speak it this way "Yes, I am working on my art degree and plan to do portraits professionally." Finally, I would act on that by taking art classes and continue crafting my skill. Eventually, I will see the positive results/success I'm looking for.

Conversely, if I think positively but speak negatively...it will cancel out. Or if I speak positively but have no positive action going on...nothing will happen.

I looked up "How Life Works" and "The Mechanics of Life" and these are really talking about the biology of how our cells work and other chemistry. TRYUNE WORKS! teaches that life is kind of like building blocks. Pick a topic you may be struggling with. See the three parts that topic consists of and then start applying them...on a consistent basis. That will help you overcome the struggle and get you back in harmony/success with how life works.

For 30+ years I was a golf instructor (by accident). My two kids had some success playing junior golf and so friends and neighbors would ask me to show them and their kids how to play golf successfully. From all of this, I got pretty good at watching golfers on the driving range and could spot right away why they were struggling with hitting bad golf shots. I was able to do that because I knew the three steps to hitting good golf shots. I learned them from studying golf and played for several decades. I "broke the code" for me so to speak.

So now you know that life works in threes. You can live your life *by choice* rather than *by chance* and that my friend... is the key to a fulfilling life.

LIFE WORKS
IN THREES!

**My sanctuary on the Pacific coast**

# Introduction

Navigating the art of time management in life is like learning to dance with the rhythm of our responsibilities and desires. It's about crafting a melody that harmonizes productivity with peace, ambition with contentment. Developing this skill begins with understanding our priorities and crafting a schedule that respects both our commitments and our need for rest and rejuvenation. It's not just about filling every minute with tasks but about crafting a balanced cadence that allows us to thrive.

In this friendly journey of time management, we discover the power of intentionality and mindfulness. By setting clear goals and breaking them down into manageable steps, we create a roadmap that guides us through the complexities of daily life. Embracing a friendly approach means being kind to ourselves amidst inevitable setbacks and recognizing that each day offers new opportunities for growth and learning. It involves celebrating progress, no matter how small, and learning from moments when our plans veer off course.

Furthermore, cultivating the skill of managing time in a friendly tone encourages us to cultivate habits that nourish our well-being. It's about finding joy in the process of accomplishment rather than merely chasing after deadlines. By fostering a positive relationship with time, we cultivate resilience and adaptability, knowing that each moment is an opportunity to make meaningful choices that align with our values and aspirations. Ultimately, it's not just about managing minutes and hours but about crafting a life that feels fulfilling and balanced, where our time serves as a tool for personal growth and connection with others.

# My discovery of the Tryune Concept

Before we dive into time struggles and how to overcome them, let me share my discovery of the Tryune Concept and how life works in threes. It all began in the summer of 1982.

I grew up with parents who treated everyone with decency and respect. My three older sisters and I were raised in a home that was "middle-class traditional." We lived in modest homes in different small towns, attended school and church on a regular basis and celebrated all the traditional holidays. Eventually we settled during the spring of 1964 in the big city of Houston, Texas. I'll never forget the vastness of the city and hearing sirens from police cars, fire trucks and ambulances on a regular basis. I was excited and scared at the same time.

Once settled in this fast-paced city, I finished my growing-up years with an academic diploma and sweetheart intact. I got a job, bought a car, got married, bought a house and produced two beautiful babies in a span of about 5 years. Talk about having to grow up fast!

Things went from great in my childhood to absolute misery in my young adulthood. I began to struggle with my job because deep down I just hated what I was doing. This problem created a snowball effect because soon after, my weight, my finances, my relationships, my happiness and everything else worth saving was going down the drain. I eventually hit a level of frustration that I had never experienced before and didn't know how to get out of it. My cry for help was for anyone or anything to come to my rescue. I just ran out of solutions for my situation.

*This is when my discovery happened.*

One night shortly after my meltdown, while sleeping soundly, the word "triune" began to softly pound in my head like a mantra. I woke up a little startled and decided to go look up the word in my favorite dictionary (this was WAY before Google.) The definition said '**triune** (try-une) – 1) a group of three things; united. 2) Being 3 in 1 such as *humans are mental, physical and spiritual.* I scratched my head, got a glass of water and went back to bed.

The next day while driving around town, I began thinking about things that I was taught in my younger years that came in threes. My Boy Scout manual taught that to have **character**, I needed to be *1) physically strong, 2) mentally awake and 3) morally straight.* My high school football coach would say emphatically "If you want to be **a good football player**, you have to be *1) mobile 2) agile and 3) hostile!*" My first sales manager shared with me that to be **a successful salesman**, I needed to have *1) sales skills, 2) product knowledge and 3) a good image.*

"Hmm", I thought, "wonder if there are other examples out there of things that work in threes?" So, some 40 years later, I have researched and discovered that many, many things work in threes. What this message was telling me is that to achieve success or balance in any significant area of my life, the three things that area consisted of had to be present continuously. That's when I had my epiphany. This discovery was telling me the secret to how life <u>really</u> works.

*Tryune is a play on the word "triune" as an invitation to "try" this concept. Furthermore, we do not say that life <u>only</u> works in threes. Life also works in ones, twos, fours and so on. What has been observed though is that the many things significant to life, just so happen to come and work in threes. That's what is being shared in this book.*

Now, you are about to see 40+ years of research and proof that life works in threes. I did not make up any of these topics. I invite you to research them on the internet to validate what is written here. There are some interesting facts that most of us have never realized...until now.

# How Life Works in Threes (around 200 examples)

<u>**LIFE**</u>

**Humans consist of** *body, mind and soul.*

**A human's basic needs** are *health, income and provisions.*

**A human's basic wants** are *comfort, gain and approval.*

**Our minds are made up of** the *conscious, the subconscious and the unconscious.*

**Philosophy explains** *the id, the ego and superego.*

**Atoms** consist of *protons, neutrons and electrons.*

**Motion** is explained by *three basic laws.*

**Science** falls under three main branches: *natural, social and formal sciences*

**Time** is *past, present and future...*at the same time.

**Electricity** consists of *ohms, amperes and voltage.*

**Music's basic elements** are *duration, pitch and timbre.*

**Democracy** is a government *of the people, by the people and for the people.*

**U.S. branches of government** are *the judicial, the executive and the legislative.*

**Armed Forces** protect us on *land, air and sea.*

**Environmentally,** we are asked *to reduce, recycle and re-use.*

**The news program** gives us *the news, sports and conditions.*

**Our days** consist of *morning, afternoon and evening.*

**Three months** in each season of the year

**Our main meals** are known as *breakfast, lunch and dinner.*

**A balanced diet** consists of *good proteins, carbohydrates and fats.*

**Traditional Family consists of** *father, mother, and child(ren)*

## <u>SCIENCES</u>

**Three major branches of natural science** – *(physical, earth/space and life sciences)*

**Three major branches of modern physics** - *(classical, relativistic, quantum)*

**Three major branches of biology** *(botany, zoology, microbiology)*

**Three spatial dimensions**: *height* (up/down), *width* (left/right) and *depth* (forwards/backwards)

**Three-gauge bosons** (photon, gluon, W&Z bosons)

**Three types of elementary particles** *(leptons, quarks, gauge bosons)*

**Three quarks in every proton** *(two "up" and one "down")*

**Three primary colors of light** *(red, green, blue)*

**Three color tone properties** *(hue, value, chroma)*

**Three laws of motion** (*Newton's laws*)

**Three laws of planetary motion** (*Kepler's laws*)

**Three layers of the Sun's interior** (*core, radiative zone, convective zone*)

**Three layers of the Sun's atmosphere** (*photosphere, chromosphere, corona*)

**Three types of meteorites** (*iron, stony iron, stony*)

**Three types of galaxy shapes** (*elliptical, spiral, irregular*)

**Three substances of the universe** (*normal matter, 'dark matter', 'dark energy'*)

**Three phases of the moon** (*new moon, first quarter, full moon*)

**Three planetary regions** (*temperate, sub-tropical, tropical*)

**Three layers of the Earth** (*crust, mantle, core*)

**Three components of an ecosystem** (*producers, consumers, decomposers*)

**Three types of rocks** (*igneous, sedimentary, metamorphic*)

**Three types of fossil fuels** (*coal, crude oil, natural gas*)

**Three hydrological processes** (*evaporation, condensation, precipitation*)

**Three basic types of (meteorological) precipitation** (*liquid, freezing, frozen*)

**Three types of substances** *(mono-constituent, multi-constituent, UVCB)*

**Three phases of (normal) matter** *(solid, liquid, gas)*

**Three types of covalent chemical bonds** *(single, double and triple bonds)*

**Three isotopes of hydrogen** *(protium, deuterium, tritium)*

**Three atoms in each molecule of water** *(two hydrogen atoms and an oxygen atom)*

**Three endings to salts** *(-ide, -ite, -ate)*

**Three requirements for fire** *(fuel, oxygen, heat)*

**Three nucleotide bases** in a genetic codon

**Three domains of life** *(archaea, bacteria and eukaryotes)*

**Three major groups of flowering plants** *(monocots, eudicots, magnolids)*

**Three major functions that are basic to plant growth and development**: *(photosynthesis* [making sugars], *respiration* [metabolizing those sugars], and *transpiration* [water vapor loss]

**Three things that the chlorophyll in plants needs for photosynthesis to take place:** *(sunlight, carbon dioxide and water)*

**Transpiration serves three roles**: *(cooling the plant, moving minerals* and *sugars through the plant*, and *maintaining the turgidity pressure* [stiffness] *of the plant's cells)*

**Three parts of an insect's body** *(head, thorax, abdomen)*

## <u>BIOLOGY</u>

**Three types of cones in the retina**, relating to the three primary colors

**Three semi-circular canals in the ear** *(lateral, anterior, posterior)*

**Three sections in the ear** *(outer, middle, inner)*

**Three ossicles in the middle ear** *(malleus, incus, stapes)*

**Three segments to each limb** *(proximal, mid, distal)*

**Three bones in each arm** *(humerus, radius, ulna)*

**Three joints in the arm** *(shoulder, elbow, wrist)*

**Three joints in the leg** *(hip, knee, ankle)*

**Three joints in the elbow** *(humeroulnar, humeroradial, proximal radioulnar)*

**Three functional compartments in the knee joint** *(the femoropatellar, medial femorotibial* and *lateral femorotibial articulations)*

**Three types of fibrous joints** *(sutures, gomphoses, syndesmoses)*

**Three types of bone in each hand** (*carpals, metacarpals, phalanges*)

**Three types of bone in each foot** (*tarsals, metatarsals, phalanges*)

**Three bones (phalanges) in each finger and in each toe** (*proximal, intermediate, distal*)

**Three layers of skin** (*dermis, epidermis, hypodermis*)

**Three components of a cell** (*cell membrane, nucleus, cytoplasm*)

**Three types of blood vessels** (*arteries, veins, capillaries*)

**Three types of blood cells** [*red* (erythrocytes), *white* (leukocytes), *platelets* (thrombocytes)]

**Three processes of the intestinal tract** (*ingestion, digestion, excretion*)

**Three germ layers** (*Endoderm, Mesoderm, Ectoderm*)

**Three parts of a human tooth** (*crown, neck, root*)

**Three organs of otolaryngology** (*ear, nose, throat*)

**Three major body systems** (*digestive, circulatory, respiratory*)

**Three parts to a neuron:** (*soma* [*cell body*], *axon, dendrites*)

**Three main parts of the brain** (*forebrain, midbrain, hindbrain*)

**Three parts of the forebrain** (*cerebrum, thalamus, hypothalamus*)

**Three parts of the midbrain** (*colliculi, tegmentum, cerebral peduncles*)

**Three parts of the hindbrain** (*cerebellum, pons, medulla*)

**Three membranes enclosing the brain** (*dura mater, arachnoid, pia mater*)

**The brain operates on three levels:** *consciously* (for cognitive thought and declarative memory); *subconsciously* (for pre-planned actions and procedural memory); and *unconsciously* (for breathing, heart beating, etc.)

**Our conscious mind is fed from three sources**: *our senses* (which can be fooled); *our memory* (which is flawed); and *our imagination* (which is inventive)

**Three aspects of the human mind** (*memory, intellect, will*)

**Three parts of the human personality** (*id, ego, superego*)

**The sum of human capacity consists of three abilities** (*thought, word and deed*)

**Three times of man** (*birth, life, death*)

**Three periods of the Gait Cycle** (*initial double limb support, single limb support, and terminal double limb support*)

## <u>MUSIC</u>

**Three types of musical notes** (*sharps, flats, naturals*)

**Three aspects of a song** (*lyrics, melody, rhythm*)

**Three types of musical chords** (*root, third, fifth*)

## MATHEMATICS

**Three types of a real number** (*positive, negative, zero*)

**Three parts to any arithmetic operation**: for addition: *augend, addend and sum* - for subtraction: *minuend, subtrahend and difference* - for multiplication: *multiplicand, multiplier and product* - for division: *dividend, divisor and quotient*

**Three laws of arithmetic operations** (*commutative, associative, distributive*)

**Three types of equivalence relation** (*reflexivity, symmetry, transitivity*)

**Three types of symmetry operations** (*translation, rotation, reflection*)

**Three geometries** (*Euclidean, spherical, hyperbolic*)

**The number 3 is the basis of an entire branch of mathematics, called trigonometry** (from the Greek *trigonon* "triangle" + *metron* "measure")

**Three trigonometric functions** (*sine, cosine, tangent*)

**Three types of average** (*mean, mode, median*)

## GRAMMAR

**Three logical operators** (*AND, OR and NOT*)

**Three laws of logic** (*identity, noncontradiction, excluded middle*)

**Three parts of a logical syllogism** (*major premise, minor premise, conclusion*)

**Three grammatical parts to a sentence** (*subject, verb, complement*)

**Three persons in grammar** [*1st person* (I/we), *2nd* (you or your), *3rd* (he/she/it/they)]

**Three genders in grammar** [*masculine* (he/him), *feminine* (she/her), *neuter* (it)]

**Three forms of comparison in grammar** [*positive, comparative* (more, -er), *superlative* (most, -est)]

**Three cases in (English) grammar** [*subjective/nominative* (he), *objective/accusative* (him) and *possessive/genitive* (his)]

**Three parts of a narrative** (*beginning, middle, end*)

**Components of an essay** (*introduction, body, conclusion*)

**Elements of a rhetorical appeal** (*ethos, pathos, logos*)

**Aspects of a story** (*plot, characters, setting*)

## <u>RELIGION</u>

**The Creator** – *omniscient, omnipotent, omnipresent*

**Christian God** – *Father, Son, Holy Spirit*

**Jesus** – *The Way, The Truth, The Life*

**Ancient Near East-** *Qudshu, Astarte, Anat*

**Classical Antiquity** – Many dieties came in threes

**Hinduism** – Para Brahman is *Brahma, Visnu, Shiva*

**Ancient Celtic Cultures** – *many example of triad dieties*

**Buddhism** – *The three jewels*

**Taoism** – *The three pure ones*

**Islam** – *Fear, Hope and Love*

**Baha'i -** *Intention, Power and Action*

**Confucianism** – *Benevolence, Wisdom and Courage*

## OTHER TRIUNE EXAMPLES

**3 Coins in a Fountain**

**3 Days of the Condor**

**3 Miles in a League**

**3 Goals in a Hat Trick**

**3 Piece Suit**

**3 Feet in a Yard**

3 Books in Lord of the Rings

3 Ring Circus

3 Ships of Christopher Columbus

3 Sheets to the Wind

3 Books in a Trilogy

3 Wheels on a Tricycle

3 Wise Men

3-Legged Race

3 Ring Circus

3-Wheeler

3 Cornered Hat

3 Dimensional

3 Musketeers

3 R's (reading, 'riting, 'rithmatic)

3 Sides of a triangle

3 Races in the Triple Crown (horse racing)

3 Angles in a Triangle

3 Trimesters in a Pregnancy

3 Flavors in Neapolitan Ice Cream

3 Stars in Orion's belt

3 Barleycorns in an Inch

3 Hands on a Clock (with the Seconds Hand)

3 Colors in a Flag

3 Minute Egg

3 Great Pyramids at Giza

3 Holes in a Bowling Ball

3 Colors in a Set of Traffic Lights

3 Minutes in a Boxing Round

3 Teaspoons in a Tablespoon

3 Legs on a Stool

3 Monastic Vows (Obience, Stability, Conversatio Morum)

3 Body Types: Endomorph, Mesomorph, Ectomorph

3 Ring Notebooks

3 Germ layers: Endoderm, Mesoderm, Ectoderm

3 Species of Homo: Homo habilis, Homo erectus, Homo sapiens

3 Basic parts of a camera: Lens, Shutter, Sensor

3 Stages of a Project lifecycle: initiation, planning, execution

The Truth, The Whole Truth and Nothing but the Truth

Life, Liberty and the Pursuit of Happiness

Hear no Evil, See no Evil, Speak no Evil

National motto of France/Haiti: Liberty, Equality, Fraternity

Paper, Rock, Scissors

Ready, Aim, Fire

On Your mark, Get Set, Go

Olympic medals of gold, silver, bronze

Types of joints (ball & socket, hinge, pivot)

Stages of a rocket launch (launch, orbit, re-entry)

Parts of a joke (setup, delivery, punchline)

Primary components of a transistor (emitter, base, collector)

Primary components of an airplane (fuselage, wings, empennage)

Basic components of a computer: CPU, memory, storage

**Three phases in the development of technology** (*eotechnic* [*mechanical*], *paleotechnic* [*steam-powered*] and *neotechnic* [*electric-powered*]

**Communication systems require three components** (*transmitter, channel, receiver*)

The list goes on. See if you can find more examples as they are everywhere in our universe! Now that you know that life works in threes (with proof!), we can begin to apply this concept to whatever topics we want.

So, to overcome struggles with time management, we need to apply the three areas that time management consists of – PRIORITIZE, ORGANIZE and MINDFUL. Let's get started!

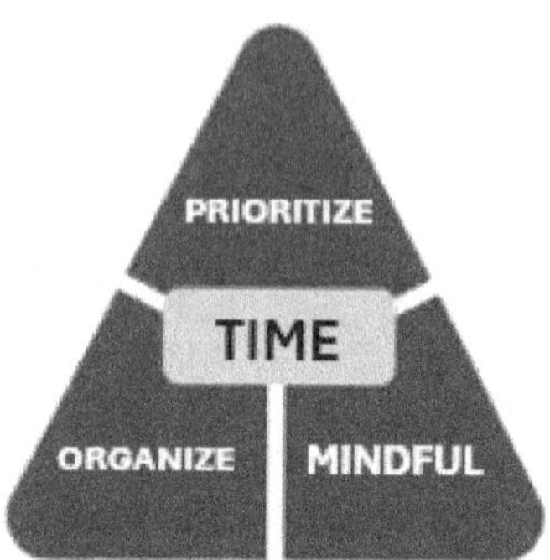
PRIORITIZE
TIME
ORGANIZE
MINDFUL

# TIME

Time, in its elusive and relentless march, has captivated human civilization since ancient times. From the earliest agrarian societies who marked the passage of seasons to the precision of modern atomic clocks, humanity has continually sought to grasp and harness time more efficiently. The concept of timekeeping evolved alongside early human societies, initially guided by natural phenomena like the movement of celestial bodies and the cycles of nature. Ancient civilizations such as the Egyptians and Babylonians developed rudimentary calendars to organize their agricultural activities and religious ceremonies, demonstrating an early recognition of the practical and spiritual importance of time.

As civilizations grew more complex, so too did their methods of time measurement. The Romans introduced the Julian calendar in 45 BCE, refining earlier lunar calendars with a solar-based system that remains the foundation of our modern Gregorian calendar. The medieval period saw the development of mechanical clocks, first appearing in European monasteries around the 13th century, which revolutionized timekeeping by providing a standardized method of measuring hours and minutes. This innovation not only facilitated more precise scheduling of religious observances but also spurred advancements in commerce, navigation, and eventually the Industrial Revolution.

The Industrial Revolution marked a watershed moment in humanity's relationship with time. As factories and railways demanded greater punctuality and efficiency, the need for synchronized timekeeping became paramount. The advent of standardized time zones in the 19th century, spearheaded by figures like Sir Sandford Fleming, further exemplified society's quest to manage time on a global scale. In the 20th century, advancements in technology led to the development of atomic clocks, the most accurate timekeeping devices ever created, which underpin modern systems such as GPS and telecommunications.

Today, as our world becomes increasingly interconnected and fast-paced, the pursuit of efficient time management remains a cornerstone of both personal productivity and societal progress.

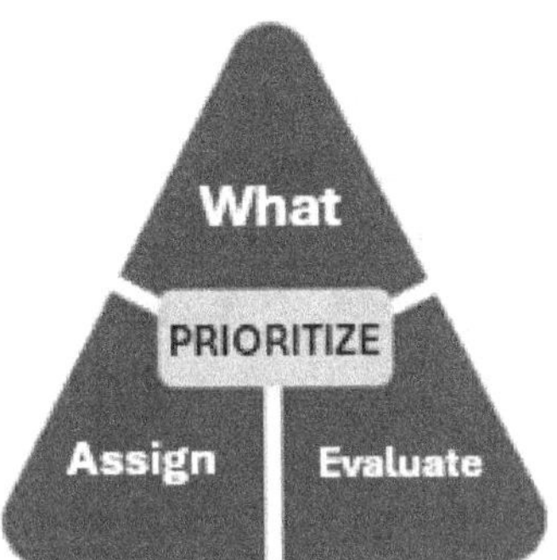

What
PRIORITIZE
Assign
Evaluate

# PRIORITIZE

Prioritizing our time is like being the curator of our own daily museum, carefully selecting which exhibits to showcase to make the most of each day. It's about recognizing that our time is finite and valuable, and how we choose to spend it shapes our experiences and outcomes. By identifying what truly matters to us—whether it's pursuing career goals, nurturing relationships, pursuing hobbies, or simply finding moments of peace—we empower ourselves to create meaningful days filled with purpose and fulfillment.

When we prioritize our time effectively, we create a framework that aligns our actions with our aspirations. It allows us to focus our energy on tasks and activities that contribute positively to our lives, rather than spreading ourselves thin across countless distractions. This friendly approach to prioritization is not about rigidly adhering to a strict schedule, but rather about making intentional choices that enhance our well-being and satisfaction. It enables us to say 'yes' to the opportunities that resonate with our values and 'no' to those that do not serve our greater purpose.

Moreover, prioritizing our time fosters a sense of empowerment and control over our lives. It helps us manage stress more effectively by reducing the overwhelm that comes from feeling pulled in multiple directions. By setting clear priorities, we gain clarity on what needs our immediate attention and what can be delegated or postponed. This clarity allows us to navigate our days with confidence, knowing that we are investing our time in ways that bring us closer to our personal and professional goals. Ultimately, prioritizing our time in a friendly tone is about honoring ourselves and our aspirations, creating space for growth, joy, and fulfillment in each day we live.

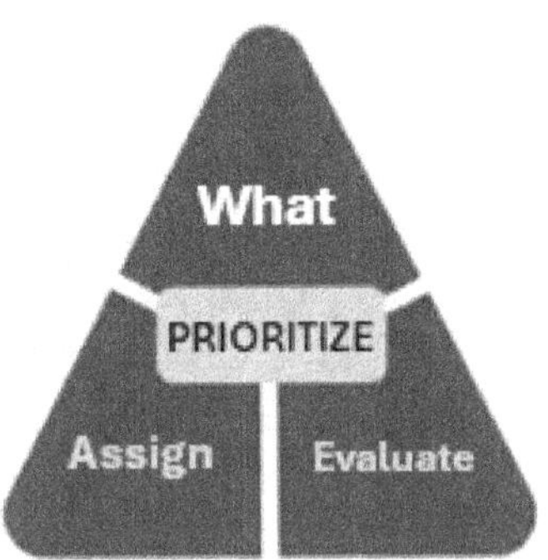
What
PRIORITIZE
Assign
Evaluate

# What

Identifying what truly matters versus what doesn't quite make the cut is like sorting through a treasure trove to find the gems that sparkle most brightly. It's about recognizing that our time and energy are precious resources that deserve to be invested wisely. When we prioritize what is genuinely important to us—whether it's personal growth, meaningful relationships, career aspirations, or hobbies—we cultivate a sense of purpose and fulfillment in our daily lives. This friendly approach to identification is rooted in self-awareness and clarity, guiding us to make decisions that align with our values and long-term happiness.

Conversely, acknowledging what isn't as crucial allows us to release the pressure of trying to do it all. It frees up mental space and resources, enabling us to focus more deeply on our priorities. This doesn't mean neglecting responsibilities or ignoring lesser tasks entirely, but rather approaching them with a balanced perspective. By understanding their relative importance, we can allocate appropriate time and effort, maintaining efficiency without sacrificing our well-being.

Moreover, distinguishing between what is truly important and what is less so promotes authenticity and personal growth. It encourages us to nurture relationships that bring joy and support, pursue activities that ignite passion, and strive for goals that resonate deeply with our aspirations. This friendly sorting process empowers us to lead more fulfilling lives, where each day becomes an opportunity to invest in what matters most to us. By embracing this clarity, we cultivate resilience and focus, navigating life's complexities with a sense of purpose and inner harmony.

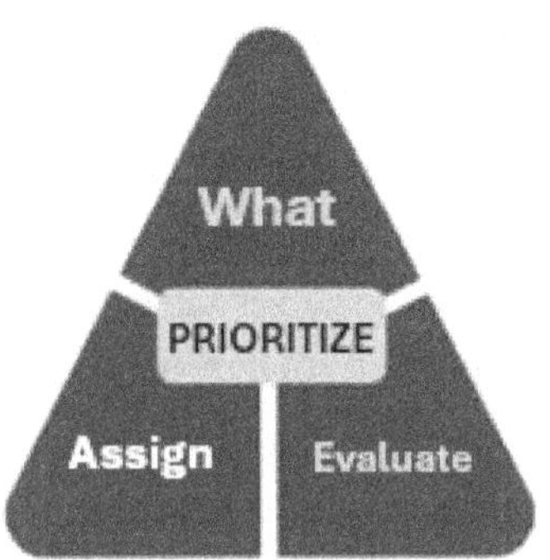

What
PRIORITIZE
Assign
Evaluate

# Assign

Assigning priorities to tasks—deciding what needs to be done first, secondly, or thirdly—is akin to crafting a roadmap for our day that leads to success with a smile. It's about applying wisdom to our time management, ensuring that we tackle tasks in an order that maximizes productivity and minimizes stress. By categorizing tasks based on urgency, importance, and impact, we create a structured approach that guides us through our responsibilities with clarity and efficiency.

In this friendly journey of prioritization, we learn to distinguish between tasks that are time-sensitive and those that contribute most significantly to our goals. By addressing urgent tasks first, we mitigate the risk of missing deadlines or causing unnecessary pressure on ourselves. This approach fosters a sense of accomplishment and momentum, setting a positive tone for the rest of the day's endeavors.

Furthermore, assigning tasks in a thoughtful sequence allows us to optimize our energy levels and mental focus. By tackling more demanding or complex tasks when our concentration is at its peak, we increase our likelihood of achieving high-quality results. This friendly strategy also includes scheduling breaks and moments of relaxation between tasks, promoting sustainable productivity and preventing burnout. It's about respecting our natural rhythms and maintaining a balanced approach to our workload, ensuring that each task receives the attention and effort it deserves.

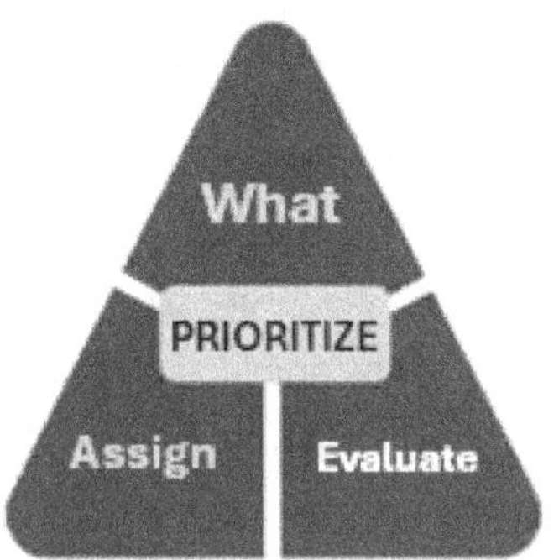

What
PRIORITIZE
Assign
Evaluate

# Evaluate

Evaluating your to-do list at the end of your day, week, or month is like taking a gentle stroll through the garden of your accomplishments. It's a moment to pause, reflect, and celebrate the progress you've made, while also preparing for the next steps ahead. This friendly evaluation process is not just about checking off tasks; it's about gaining insights into your productivity patterns, learning from your experiences, and refining your approach to time management.

At the end of each day, reviewing your to-do list allows you to acknowledge what you've achieved and identify any tasks that may need to be carried over to the next day. This practice fosters a sense of closure, helping you transition from work mode to relaxation or personal time with a clear mind. It also provides an opportunity to recognize your efforts, no matter how small, and to cultivate gratitude for the progress made.

On a weekly or monthly basis, evaluating your to-do list takes on a broader perspective. It enables you to assess your overall productivity and accomplishments over a longer period. By reviewing completed tasks, identifying recurring priorities, and adjusting goals as needed, you refine your strategy for future planning. This friendly review process empowers you to prioritize effectively, allocate resources wisely, and maintain a healthy balance between work and personal life.

Moreover, this chore of evaluation serves as a valuable learning experience. It encourages self-reflection and continuous improvement, allowing you to recognize patterns of efficiency and areas where you can grow. By approaching this evaluation with a friendly tone—free from self-judgment or harsh criticism—you create a supportive environment for personal and professional development. It's about fostering a positive relationship with your to-do list, using it as a tool to guide your journey towards achieving your aspirations with clarity, purpose, and a sense of accomplishment.

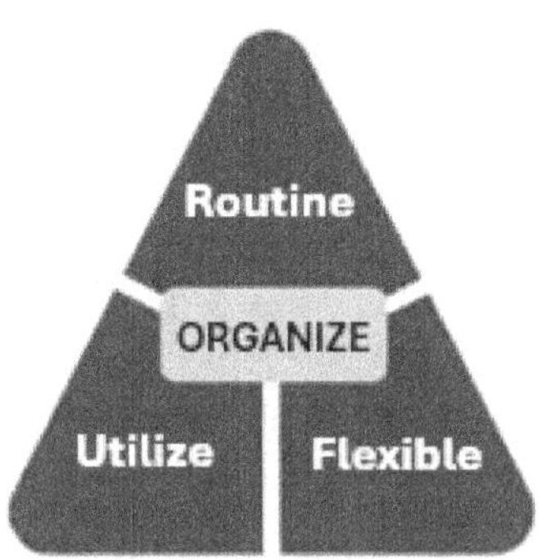
Routine
ORGANIZE
Utilize
Flexible

## ORGANIZE

Organizing your time on a regular basis is like tending to a garden—you nurture it with care and attention to ensure it flourishes. The first key to effective time organization is establishing a routine. By setting aside dedicated time each day or week to plan and prioritize tasks, you create a framework for productivity and success. This friendly approach to routine allows you to start each day with clarity and purpose, knowing exactly what needs to be accomplished and how it aligns with your goals.

The second key involves utilizing tools and techniques that work best for you. Whether it's a digital calendar, a traditional planner, task management apps, or a combination of these, finding tools that suit your preferences and lifestyle enhances your organizational efforts. This friendly exploration allows you to experiment with different methods until you discover what helps you stay on track and motivated. Embracing these tools with a positive mindset fosters a sense of empowerment, making it easier to stay organized amidst life's inevitable twists and turns.

Lastly, maintaining flexibility is crucial in organizing your time in a friendly manner. While structure is essential, being adaptable allows you to respond to unexpected events or changes in priorities without feeling overwhelmed. This approach encourages a balanced perspective, where you can adjust your plans as needed without sacrificing your overall productivity or well-being. Embracing flexibility with kindness towards yourself ensures that your organizational efforts remain sustainable and supportive of your personal growth and happiness.

In essence, organizing your time on a regular basis in a friendly tone revolves around establishing a routine, leveraging effective tools, and embracing flexibility. These keys empower you to navigate life's demands with confidence and clarity, ensuring that each day is a step forward towards achieving your goals while maintaining a sense of balance and well-being.

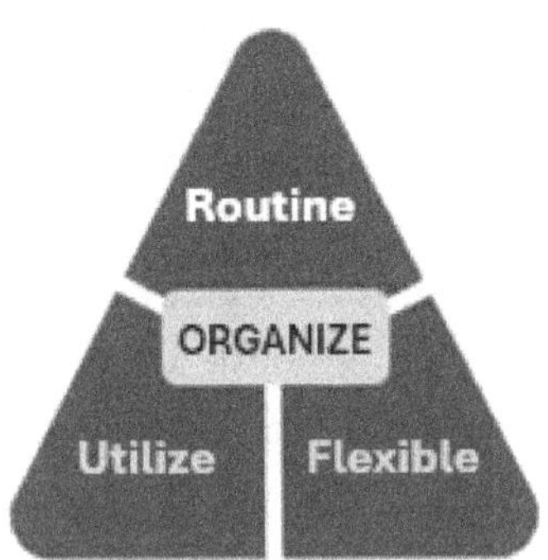
Routine
ORGANIZE
Utilize
Flexible

# Routine

Having a routine while managing your time offers a friendly structure that anchors your day in consistency and purpose. One of the key benefits is that it reduces decision fatigue by automating certain aspects of your schedule. When you establish a regular rhythm for tasks like waking up, exercising, working, and winding down, you free up mental space for more important decisions. This friendly approach allows you to approach each day with clarity and focus, knowing that your routine supports your overall well-being and productivity.

Another advantage of having a routine is that it promotes efficiency and productivity. By allocating specific time slots for different activities, you optimize your workflow and minimize distractions. This friendly organization of time enables you to complete tasks more effectively, whether it's tackling work projects, pursuing personal interests, or spending quality time with loved ones. It also fosters a sense of accomplishment as you consistently make progress towards your goals within a structured framework.

Moreover, a routine can enhance your mental and emotional well-being. It provides a sense of stability and predictability in an otherwise chaotic world, reducing stress and anxiety. This friendly consistency allows you to manage your energy levels more effectively, ensuring that you have ample time for rest, relaxation, and self-care. By incorporating activities that bring you joy and fulfillment into your routine, such as hobbies or mindfulness practices, you create a balanced lifestyle that supports both your professional success and personal happiness.

In essence, embracing a routine while managing your time in a friendly tone offers numerous benefits. It streamlines decision-making, boosts productivity, and enhances overall well-being by providing structure and stability to your day-to-day life. By cultivating a routine that aligns with your priorities and values, you create a foundation for success and fulfillment, ensuring that each day is lived with intention and purpose.

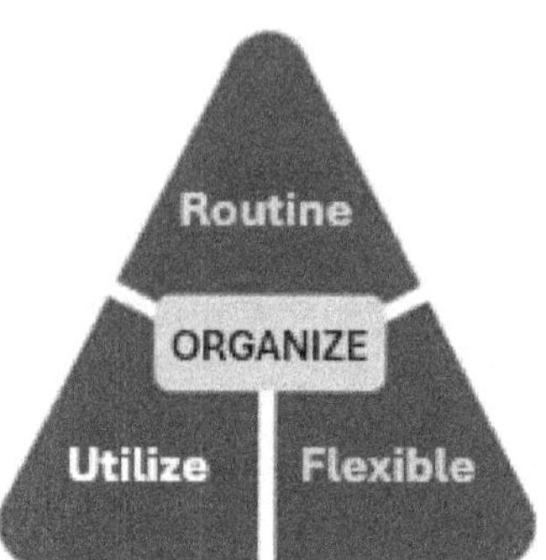
Routine
ORGANIZE
Utilize
Flexible

# Utilize

Utilizing the tools and techniques available today for managing our time offers a friendly gateway to enhanced productivity and well-being. One of the key benefits is the accessibility and convenience of digital tools. From calendar apps that sync across devices to task management platforms that streamline collaboration, these tools simplify the process of organizing tasks and priorities. This friendly integration of technology allows us to stay organized and on track with minimal effort, freeing up mental space for creativity and relaxation.

Another advantage of leveraging modern time management tools is their ability to improve efficiency and effectiveness. With features like reminders, notifications, and time tracking capabilities, these tools help us stay accountable to our goals and deadlines. This friendly support system enables us to prioritize tasks, allocate resources, and monitor progress in real-time, ensuring that we make the most of our time and efforts. Whether it's managing work projects, household chores, or personal commitments, these tools empower us to achieve more with less stress.

Moreover, utilizing time management tools fosters collaboration and teamwork, both in professional and personal settings. Shared calendars, project management software, and communication platforms facilitate seamless coordination among team members, enhancing productivity and collective achievement. This friendly collaboration ensures that everyone is on the same page regarding tasks and deadlines, promoting a supportive environment where ideas can thrive and goals can be achieved efficiently.

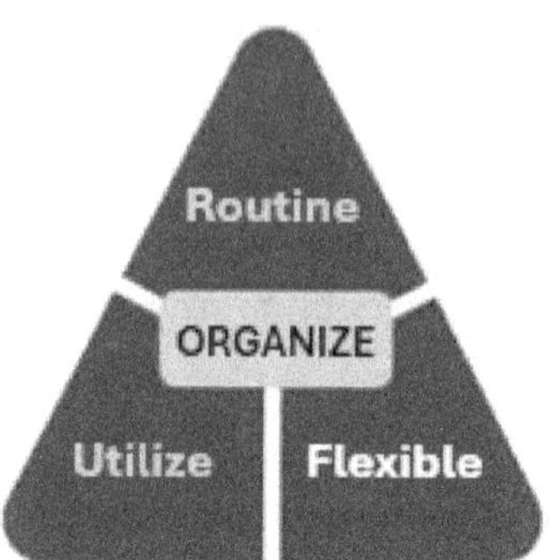

Routine
ORGANIZE
Utilize
Flexible

# Flexible

Remaining flexible when managing our time is crucial for maintaining a friendly and balanced approach to productivity and well-being. One of the key benefits of flexibility is the ability to adapt to unexpected changes and challenges. Life often throws curveballs that can disrupt even the most carefully planned schedules. By cultivating a mindset of flexibility, we can navigate these uncertainties with grace and resilience. This friendly adaptability allows us to adjust our priorities and timelines as needed, ensuring that we can still make progress towards our goals without becoming overwhelmed or discouraged.

Moreover, embracing flexibility fosters creativity and innovation. When we allow ourselves room to explore different approaches and experiment with new ideas, we open up opportunities for growth and improvement. This friendly openness to change encourages us to think outside the box, explore new possibilities, and seize opportunities that may not have been part of our original plan. It enables us to discover solutions that are more efficient, effective, and aligned with our values and aspirations.

Furthermore, remaining flexible in our time management practices promotes mental and emotional well-being. Rigidity can lead to stress and burnout as we strive to adhere strictly to schedules or expectations. This friendly flexibility, on the other hand, promotes a healthy balance between productivity and self-care. It allows us to prioritize moments of rest, relaxation, and personal fulfillment alongside our professional and personal responsibilities. By listening to our needs and adjusting our plans accordingly, we ensure that our time is spent in ways that nourish our overall happiness and satisfaction.

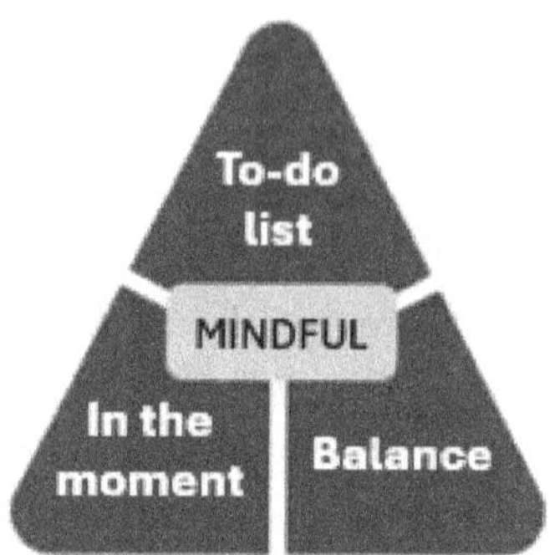

To-do
list
MINDFUL
In the
moment
Balance

# MINDFUL

Mindful time management is all about finding that sweet spot where productivity meets peace of mind. Here are the three keys to help you navigate this:

1. **Awareness of Priorities**: Start by knowing what truly matters to you. List out your top priorities in life, whether it's family time, career goals, personal health, or hobbies. This awareness will guide how you allocate your time.
2. **Present Moment Focus**: Stay grounded in the here and now. When you're working on a task or spending time with loved ones, give it your full attention. Avoid multitasking and distractions that pull you away from being fully present.
3. **Balanced Scheduling**: Create a schedule that respects both your commitments and your need for rest and rejuvenation. Mindful time management isn't just about packing your day full; it's about finding a healthy balance that sustains your energy and well-being.

By integrating these keys into your daily life, you'll find yourself not just managing time, but living it

To-do
list
MINDFUL
In the
moment
Balance

# To-Do List

Having a to-do list is like having a superpower for managing your time effectively! Here are some awesome benefits that come with this simple yet powerful tool:

Firstly, a to-do list keeps you organized and on track. It's like a roadmap for your day or week, outlining what needs to be done and when. By jotting down tasks, whether big projects or small errands, you're less likely to forget anything important. Plus, crossing items off your list gives you a satisfying sense of accomplishment—talk about motivation!

Secondly, it helps you prioritize like a pro. You can rank tasks based on urgency and importance, ensuring you tackle what matters most first. This way, you're not just busy; you're productive. Whether it's finishing that report due tomorrow or making time for a workout, your to-do list helps you allocate your precious time wisely.

Lastly, and perhaps most importantly, a to-do list reduces stress and boosts focus. Instead of trying to remember everything in your head (which can be overwhelming), you can relax knowing it's all written down. This frees up mental space for creativity and problem-solving. Plus, as you work through your list, you can see your progress unfold—making even the busiest days feel more manageable.

So, whether you're a seasoned list-maker or just getting started, harness the power of a to-do list to supercharge your time management skills. It's not just a tool; it's your secret weapon for a more organized, productive, and stress-free life!

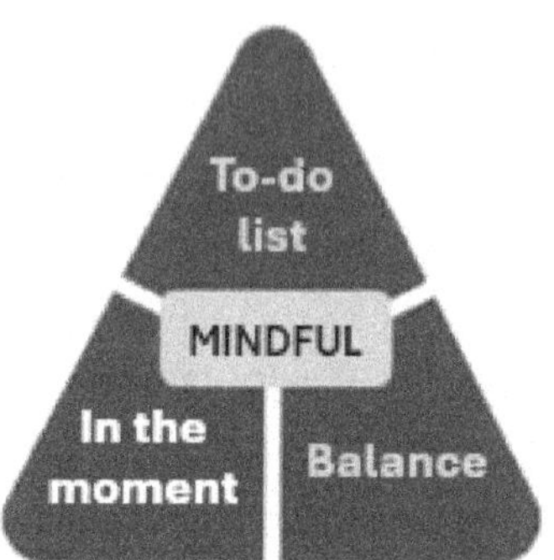
To-do list
MINDFUL
In the moment
Balance

# In The Moment

Living in the moment is like savoring the juiciest slice of life—it's all about being fully present and engaged with whatever you're doing, especially when managing your time. Here's why it's so important:

Firstly, being present enhances your focus and productivity. When you're fully immersed in the task at hand, whether it's a work project or spending time with loved ones, you're able to give it your undivided attention. This heightened focus not only improves the quality of your work but also helps you accomplish tasks more efficiently. By resisting the urge to multitask or dwell on past mistakes, you free up mental energy to tackle what's in front of you right now.

Secondly, living in the moment fosters a deeper appreciation for life's experiences. Instead of rushing through tasks just to check them off your list, take a moment to breathe and savor each activity. Whether it's enjoying a quiet cup of coffee in the morning or going for a walk in nature, being present allows you to fully immerse yourself in the richness of the moment. This mindfulness not only reduces stress but also cultivates a sense of gratitude for the little joys that make life meaningful.

Lastly, embracing the present moment promotes better decision-making and time management. When you're aware of the here and now, you're better equipped to make informed choices about how to allocate your time and resources. This means prioritizing activities that align with your values and long-term goals, rather than getting caught up in distractions or worrying about the future. By grounding yourself in the present, you become more intentional about how you spend your time, ultimately leading to a more balanced and fulfilling life.

So, as you navigate the hustle and bustle of daily life, remember to pause, breathe, and embrace the present moment. It's not just about managing your time—it's about living it with purpose and joy.

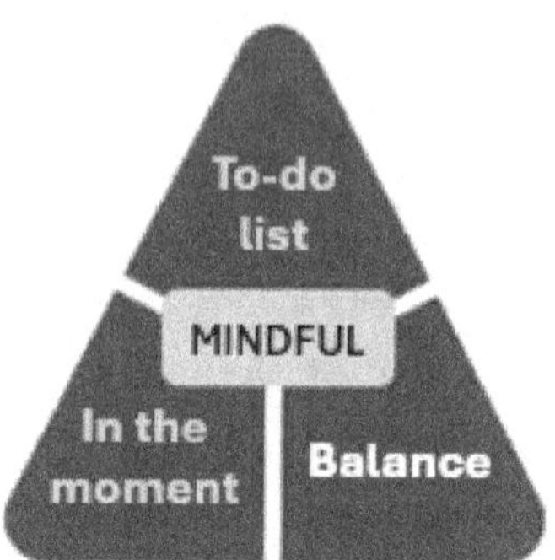
To-do
list
MINDFUL
In the
moment
Balance

# Balance

Maintaining a healthy balance while tackling your to-do list each day is like finding the perfect rhythm in a dance—it's all about harmony and flow. Here's why it's wise to strike that balance:

Firstly, balancing your to-do list prevents burnout and preserves your well-being. It's easy to get caught up in the whirlwind of tasks, but remember, you're not a superhero (even though you might feel like one sometimes!). Incorporating breaks, both short pauses between tasks and longer moments of relaxation, allows you to recharge and approach your tasks with renewed energy and focus. This mindful approach ensures you're not just racing through your list but maintaining your physical and mental health along the way.

Secondly, a balanced approach helps you prioritize effectively. Not all tasks are created equal, and some may have a greater impact on your goals or well-being than others. By taking a step back and assessing your to-do list with a clear mind, you can identify which tasks truly deserve your immediate attention and which can be delegated, postponed, or even eliminated. This strategic thinking ensures that you're investing your time and effort where it matters most, rather than spreading yourself too thin across less significant tasks.

Lastly, maintaining balance fosters sustainability and long-term success. Consistency is key in achieving your goals, whether they're professional milestones, personal aspirations, or simply maintaining a harmonious lifestyle. By pacing yourself and balancing productivity with self-care, you're more likely to sustain momentum over time. This steady progress not only prevents burnout but also builds resilience and endurance, positioning you for continued success in both your professional and personal endeavors.

So, as you tackle your to-do list each day, remember to dance to the beat of balance. It's not just about getting things done—it's about doing them in a way that supports your well-being and sets you up for sustained achievement and happiness.

What
PRIORITIZE
Assign
Evaluate
TIME
Routine
ORGANIZE
Utilize
Flexible
To-do list
MINDFUL
In the
moment
Balance

# SUMMARY

Living in today's fast-paced world can feel like navigating a whirlwind of cell phones, social media, and economic challenges. It's a balancing act that many of us face daily. Here's a friendly take on the challenges and how to navigate them:

Firstly, cell phones and social media have revolutionized how we connect and consume information. While they bring convenience and connectivity, they also introduce distractions and pressures to constantly stay plugged in. Finding a healthy balance involves setting boundaries—whether it's turning off notifications during family time or scheduling regular breaks from screens. By reclaiming moments of unplugged peace, you can regain focus and reconnect with what truly matters.

Secondly, tough economic times can create stress and uncertainty. Whether it's navigating job instability or managing finances in a volatile market, these challenges can weigh heavily. However, it's important to remember resilience. Seeking support from friends, family, or professional networks can provide valuable perspective and resources. Additionally, focusing on personal growth and adaptability can empower you to weather economic storms and emerge stronger.

Lastly, amidst the chaos, practicing mindfulness can be a beacon of calm. Mindfulness encourages living in the present moment, appreciating life's simple pleasures, and managing stress effectively. Techniques like deep breathing, meditation, or simply taking a mindful walk can help center your mind and reduce anxiety. By cultivating mindfulness, you can navigate the complexities of modern life with greater clarity, resilience, and a sense of inner peace.

In conclusion, while the modern world presents its challenges, it also offers opportunities for growth and connection. By setting boundaries with technology, seeking support during tough times, and practicing mindfulness, you can navigate life's chaos with grace and resilience.

Remember, it's okay to unplug, seek help when needed, and prioritize your well-being in this fast-paced journey we're all on together.

# Invitation

When I was a youngster back in the 50s, 60s and 70s, life was pretty simple. But since then, all of these technological advances with smart phones and computers have sped life up considerably. You would think with better life tools that our lives would get simpler not more hectic. But alas, it is the world we live in.

What I found, for me, was that I had a choice to make. I either continue trying to keep up with technological advances or surrender all of that and live the way that works for me. I chose the latter. We all have 24 hours in a day. Eight hours are devoted to sleeping and another eight to working. That leaves eight hours left to do what I choose with it. Well...I gotta eat, so a couple of hours for breakfast, lunch and dinner. Now we're down to about five hours...you get the point.

Being selfish with my time has allowed me to keep my sanity. Trying to social media and other latest trends proved to exhausting and time-consuming for me. I gotta have my rest and I gotta work so I can eat and rest. The other stuff, as the Italians say, "Fuhgeddaboudit!"

So, my invitation is...be selfish with your time and don't allow others to waste it. That's what other people want from you, your time and money. Guard them with your life.

*When you're with someone who is sharing their struggles with you...just smile at him/her and give them one of these. He/she will ask "What is that?" Then simply reply "Life Works in Threes."*

# Other titles coming out:

- Weight Struggles?
- Abundance Struggles?
- Parenting Struggles?
- Life Struggles?
- Purpose Struggles?
- Happiness Struggles?
- Sales Struggles?
- Speaker Struggles?
- Romance Struggles?
- Network Struggles?
- Marriage Struggles?
- Divorce Struggles?
- Money Struggles?
- Career Struggles?
- Dating Struggles?
- Caretaker Struggles?
- Forgiveness Struggles?
- Grieving Struggles?
- Success Struggles?
- Golf Struggles?
- Workplace Struggles?
- Stress Struggles?
- Shame/Guilt Struggles?
- Addiction Struggles?

# Quotes about Time

"Time you enjoy wasting is not wasted time." - Marthe Troly-Curtin

"Time is a created thing. To say, 'I don't have time,' is like saying, 'I don't want to.'" - Lao Tzu

"Time is a great healer, but a poor beautician." - Lucille S. Harper

"Time is what keeps everything from happening at once." - Ray Cummings

“No need for a watch. Just look at the sky. It's either morning time, midday time or evening time. Simple.” - Unknown

*Remember,*

*When you get right down to it,*

*Life is about making choices.*

*Every day, all day long, that's what we do.*

- *We choose to get out of bed or not.*
- *We choose to clean up or not.*
- *We choose what to eat all day.*
- *We choose to exercise or not.*
- *We choose to go to work or not.*
- *We choose to do a good job or not.*
- *We choose to come home or not.*
- *We choose to watch TV or do something constructive.*
- *We choose to bed at a decent hour or not.*

## Weekly Chore Planner Template

## Weekly Time Planner

| FOR THE WEEK OF:<br>5/29/2017<br>**TASK** | MON<br>29<br>To Do? | DONE<br>Day 1 | TUE<br>30<br>To Do? 2 | DONE<br>DAY 2 | WED<br>31<br>To Do? 3 | DONE<br>DAY 3 | THU<br>To Do? 4 | DONE<br>DAY 4 | FRI<br>2<br>To Do? 5 | DONE<br>DAY 5 |
|---|---|---|---|---|---|---|---|---|---|---|
| Pick Up Toys/Misc | | | | | | | | | | |
| Get Mail | | | | | | | | | | |
| Take Out Trash | | | | | | | | | | |
| Dinner Dishes | | | | | | | | | | |
| Dust | | | | | | | | | | |
| Sweep | | | | | | | | | | |
| Vacuum | | | | | | | | | | |
| Mop | | | | | | | | | | |
| Clean Bathroom | | | | | | | | | | |
| Clean Bedroom | | | | | | | | | | |
| Laundry | | | | | | | | | | |
| Mow Lawn | | | | | | | | | | |
| Rake Lawn | | | | | | | | | | |
| Weed Garden | | | | | | | | | | |
| Trim Hedges | | | | | | | | | | |

# Month to Month Time Planner Template



| January | February | March | July | August | September |
| --- | --- | --- | --- | --- | --- |
|  |  |  |  |  |  |

| April | May | June | October | November | December |
| --- | --- | --- | --- | --- | --- |
|  |  |  |  |  |  |

# Weekly Meal Planner Template

## Weekly Menu Planner

|  | Breakfast | Lunch | Dinner | Snacks |
|---|---|---|---|---|
| Sunday |  |  |  |  |
| Monday |  |  |  |  |
| Tuesday |  |  |  |  |
| Wednesday |  |  |  |  |
| Thursday |  |  |  |  |
| Friday |  |  |  |  |
| Saturday |  |  |  |  |

Come up with as many planners as you see fit.

Here's a list of various planner templates that can help you manage your time effectively:

**Daily Planner Template**:

Structured to plan out your day hour by hour, including tasks, appointments, and priorities.

**Weekly Planner Template**:

Allows you to plan your entire week at a glance, with sections for goals, tasks, and notes.

**Monthly Planner Template**:

Provides an overview of the month, including important dates, goals, and tasks to accomplish.

**Yearly Planner Template**:

Helps you plan major events and goals for the entire year, broken down by quarters or months.

**To-Do List Template**:

Simple list format for jotting down tasks that need to be completed, with checkboxes for tracking progress.

**Goal Tracker Template**:

Focuses on tracking specific goals over time, with milestones and progress indicators.

**Habit Tracker Template**:

Helps you establish and track daily habits or routines over a period of time.

**Project Planner Template**:

Designed to manage larger projects, including tasks, deadlines, resources, and milestones.

**Meal Planner Template**:

Allows you to plan meals for the week or month ahead, including shopping lists and recipes.

**Fitness Planner Template**:

Tracks workouts, fitness goals, progress measurements, and meal planning for a healthier lifestyle.

**Financial Planner Template:**

Helps manage budgets, savings goals, expenses, and investments.

**Travel Planner Template:**

Organizes travel itineraries, packing lists, reservations, and activities for trips.

**Study Planner Template:**

Structured to plan study sessions, assignments, exams, and academic goals.

**Social Media Content Planner Template:**

Organizes content ideas, posting schedules, and analytics for managing social media accounts.

**Reflection Journal Template:**

Provides prompts for daily or weekly reflections on achievements, challenges, and lessons learned.

*These templates can be found in various formats such as PDFs, Excel spreadsheets, or online planning tools, depending on your preference for digital or physical planning. They are designed to help you organize different aspects of your life and manage your time effectively.*

When someone is struggling with a particular area or two, chances are they are "out of balance" with how life works. How does life work? Life works in threes.

If you're interested in personal topics like life, health, money or business topics like sales, time management and public speaking...TRYUNE WORKS! can shed some light on creating success in those areas.

The definition of TRIUNE is a group of three things; united. Being three in one, such as - humans are *mental, physical* and *spiritual beings*. The word TRYUNE is a play of the word TRIUNE, encouraging all to try this concept and help eliminate struggling unnecessarily.

LifeWorksInThrees.com